The Science of Flight

by Alexandra Hanson-Harding

Table of Contents

Introduction	2
Early Science of Flight	4
Forces of Flight	8
Parts of a Plane	12
How Planes Have Changed	16
Beyond the Plane	22
Conclusion	28
Glossary	30
Index	31
Analyze the Text	32

Introduction

Flying creatures, such as birds and insects, have lived on Earth far longer than humans. People have always observed them flapping, hovering, and soaring through the sky.

Even in ancient Greece, people imagined what it would be like to fly. In a Greek myth, a man named Daedalus and his son Icarus are trapped in a tower. To escape, Daedalus makes wings of wax and feathers for himself and his son. But instead of flying straight, as his father instructed him to, Icarus flies closer and closer to the sun. The wax melts, and Icarus plunges to Earth.

For thousands of years, the idea of human flight seemed impossible—or dangerous. Authors like Edgar Allan Poe, H. G. Wells, and Jules Verne imagined both the wonder and horror of flight—the freedom to travel to unknown worlds, but the terrible destruction that could be caused by using flying machines for war. Many of their imagined innovations have become realities.

etching and model of early helicopter designs

Humans have always hungered for flight. Renaissance artist Leonardo da Vinci sketched designs for early helicopters in his notebooks. Countless others since then have contributed ideas—in fields including physics, meteorology, chemistry, and engineering—that allowed flight to become humanly possible.

Humans spent more than a century trying to master the challenge of flight. Harnessing the power of flight has transformed the way people live, think, and dream. As flight pioneer Otto Lilienthal said, "To invent an airplane is nothing. To build one is something. But to fly is everything."

Chapter 1
Early Science of Flight

Most people agree that human flight began when Wilbur Wright (1867–1912) and Orville Wright (1871–1948) made a historic flight in Kitty Hawk, North Carolina, on December 17, 1903. Before building gliders, the brothers, two bicycle mechanics from Ohio, wrote to the Smithsonian Institution in Washington, D.C. to ask for information. They studied everything they could from earlier flight pioneers.

One pioneer was Sir George Cayley (1773–1857), who has been called "the father of **aeronautics**." Cayley designed the first glider to successfully carry a human being up in the air. Modern flying machines have been designed, both in concept and in model, based on his theories about **aerodynamics**.

Another pioneer, Otto Lilienthal (1848–1896), researched the flight of birds to make gliders. After building gliders and making more than 2,000 glides, Lilienthal knew that air affects gliders' movements.

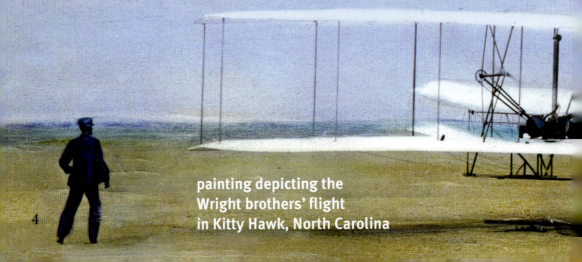

painting depicting the Wright brothers' flight in Kitty Hawk, North Carolina

Lilienthal made air charts and wrote about his discoveries. He thought he could control the air by wiggling his legs as they hung from the glider.

In 1896, while Lilienthal was carrying out trial flights with one of his gliders, the glider suddenly became caught in a gust of wind. Though he tried to maintain consistent **lift** by angling his body, his attempt failed and he fell to the ground. Lilienthal would later die from the injury he sustained in the fall (a fractured neck). His last words were, "Sacrifices must be made."

artist's rendering of Lilienthal's glider

Lilienthal's legacy would live on, however, and his last words were not in vain: his sacrifice *did* help the Wright brothers. They agreed with his ideas about the importance of air movement, and they started making and testing gliders in 1900. But eventually, finding their gliders didn't work as well as they should have, they decided Lilienthal's air charts might be flawed. Using a homemade wind tunnel, the Wright brothers painstakingly studied air movements for months. Indeed, Lilienthal's charts were inaccurate.

Chapter 1

This information helped improve their gliders. Also helpful was Wilbur's observation that birds lean into a turn, tipping one wing downward and the other upward. Instead of making plane wings stay stable and flat in the air, as other inventors were doing at the time, the brothers constructed curved wings similar to the handles of a bicycle.

Using this new design, the Wright brothers would follow Lilienthal's strategy of practicing gliding. They determined they needed to achieve a mastery of both the concept and the physical act of controlling the flight of an aircraft before installing any kind of engine.

Both bicycles and gliders were basically unstable. The rider or pilot had to create the right balance. The Wrights tried changing their wings so they could tip more easily. This helped them learn to control turns.

In 1903, the brothers built the gas-powered *Wright Flyer I*. By that time, gasoline-powered car engines had been around for nearly twenty years. The brothers took an engine and

Early Science of Flight

How the Wright Brothers' Gliders Moved

The double-decker gliders included two layers of curved wings made of lightweight fabric stiffened with netting. They were attached to wooden struts. Metal wire tied the struts together. The pilot lay flat in the glider. His movements—using his shoulders, swiveling his hips in his hip cradle, and using a hand control—allowed him to direct the aircraft's movements.

replaced many of its pieces with aluminum. They studied propellers and decided they should work as sideways wings to scoop up air and push it behind the plane. The brothers crafted propellers from spruce, a lightweight and sturdy wood, and attached them to motors with bicycle chains. Finally, they were ready. Their motor-powered aircraft was a success. The Wrights' deep understanding of flying put them far ahead in the race to master the air. The age of flight had begun.

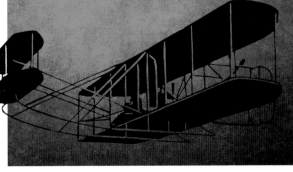

7

Chapter 2

Forces of Flight

Sir George Cayley discovered that four forces are required to make a heavier-than-air object fly. A **force** is a push or pull on an object. The push comes from the way it interacts with another object. If two objects interact, they exert forces on each other. For example, a baseball bat exerts a force when it hits a baseball.

Gravity

A plane standing still on a runway is pulled toward the center of Earth by **gravity**. The force of gravity means that smaller bodies of matter (such as a plane) are pulled toward larger bodies of matter (like Earth). But where the plane meets the ground, air resistance counteracts gravity. Air resistance prevents the plane from being pulled any farther down. The two forces act opposite to each other.

Opposing Forces

If a plane has to fight gravity even to remain on the ground, how can it possibly get off the ground? The answer is a delicate balance of the four opposing forces that Cayley determined affect all objects that are in flight. These four forces are **weight**, **thrust**, lift, and **drag**.

Weight

A plane that is on the ground is held there by the force of gravity. The measure of the force of gravity on an object is called weight. The greater the weight of an object, the more energy that is required to cause it to take flight. Because a plane is significantly heavier than air, a tremendous amount of energy must be expended to get it to move. But before a plane can go up, it must go forward.

Thrust

The action that makes a plane move forward is called thrust. Large, fuel-powered engines cause the thrust in modern airplanes. The engines pull air inward, and then push it through the end of the machine at a very fast rate. This gives the plane enough thrust to propel it forward. As it moves forward, air flows more and more quickly under its wings. With some manipulation of the plane's controls by the pilot, the plane begins to tilt upward and lifts off the ground.

Lift

Lift is the force that fights against the pull of gravity on objects. Once the plane is in the air, it will stay in the air provided that there is enough lift keeping it aloft and enough thrust moving it forward. The movement that propels the plane forward and keeps it moving is called momentum. Any moving body is said to possess momentum, or moving mass.

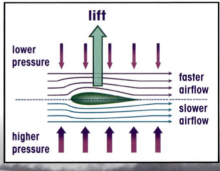

Forces of Flight

Drag

The last of the four forces that Cayley determined to have an effect on objects in flight is drag. Drag refers to certain forces that act on an object in motion. These forces act in the opposite direction of the object's velocity. For a plane that is trying to take off, drag is slowing it down by exerting force on it in the opposite direction that the plane is trying to go. During flight, drag is manipulated and induced by the wings and flaps of the plane, which give it lift and keep the plane in the air.

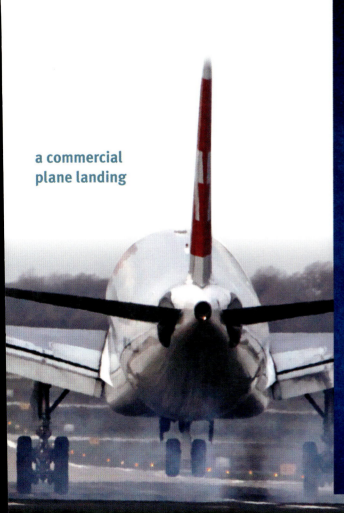

a commercial plane landing

In His Own Words

In his paper "On Aerial Navigation" published in *Nicholson's Journal of Natural Philosophy*, 1809, Cayley states: "The flight of a strong man by great muscular exertion, though a curious and interesting circumstance, in as much as it will probably be the first means of ascertaining this power, and supplying the basis whereon to improve it, would be of little use. I feel perfectly confident, however, that this noble art will soon be brought home to man's general convenience, and that we shall be able to transport ourselves and families, and their goods and chattels, more securely by air than by water, and with a velocity of from 20 to 100 miles per hour."

Chapter 3
Parts of a Plane

There are different kinds of airplanes for different purposes, but civilian passenger airplanes are the most common type of aircraft in the sky. A passenger plane has many parts that work together to allow it to defy gravity and achieve flight.

A plane's **fuselage**, or main body, is designed to be aerodynamic. The plane has a streamlined body that cuts through the air with as little drag as possible. Inside the fuselage, there is room for passengers or cargo. Also inside the front of the fuselage is the cockpit, where the pilot and copilot command the plane.

Wings are vitally important to an airplane. They give the plane lift to get up in the air, stay up, and turn in the correct direction. Wings are usually smooth, and often slightly curved from the front to the back. Wings often have extra features that help to generate lift. Slats and flaps move out from the front and rear edge of the wing during takeoff to increase lift during takeoff and landing. Jetliners have flaps on the rear edge of their wings to increase lift and drag. The flaps lie flat when the plane is at full speed, but slide back and tilt down to increase the surface and curve of the wing area when the plane is slowing down to land. Ailerons lie next to the flaps. Ailerons are similar to flaps, but their job is to push the air down on one side and up on the other, allowing the plane to turn effectively.

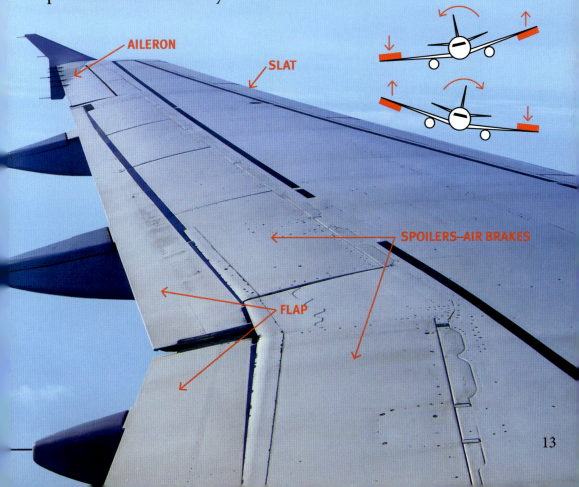

Chapter 3

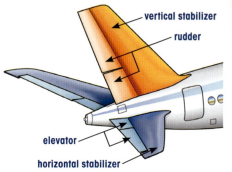

In the back of the plane are two small horizontal wings and one small vertical wing called stabilizers. The small horizontal wings have flaps called elevators—these help to change the **pitch**, or up-or-down angle, of the flight.

A rudder is a flap on the plane's vertical stabilizer. The rudder can move left or right, influencing the plane's direction.

Jet engines are another part of a plane. Airplanes pull oxygen from the air outside, and then burn it in their engines. A jet engine looks like a tube. A fan sucks air in the front. Then a compressor (a many-bladed fan) pushes the air molecules closer together to increase the air pressure. Next, fuel is sprayed into this air and ignited. The gases expand as they burn. Jets of gas shoot out the nozzle at the back. The force of the gas being expelled backward gives the plane momentum that pushes it forward.

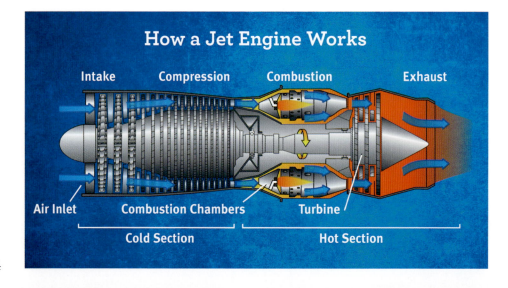

Parts of a Plane

Planes also have landing gear, spoilers, and brakes that help slow the craft down during landing. Most planes have wheels that can be tucked into their bodies during flight. When the plane approaches the runway, the wheels come out and the plane rolls smoothly to a stop.

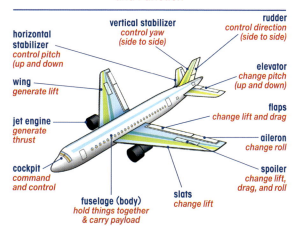

Airplane Parts Definitions and Function

- horizontal stabilizer — control pitch (up and down)
- wing — generate lift
- jet engine — generate thrust
- cockpit — command and control
- fuselage (body) — hold things together & carry payload
- vertical stabilizer — control yaw (side to side)
- rudder — control direction (side to side)
- elevator — change pitch (up and down)
- flaps — change lift and drag
- aileron — change roll
- spoiler — change lift, drag, and roll
- slats — change lift

A typical commercial plane has wheels under the nose and under the wings.

15

✈ Chapter 4
How Planes Have Changed

Planes have changed greatly since the Wright brothers' glider. During World War I, planes were initially used to gather intelligence behind the trenches of enemy lines. But as the war went on, planes started to shoot at ground troops, drop bombs, and have "dogfights" with one another with machine guns.

The First World War was the first time that militaries used planes on a large scale. Because of the rising popularity of aircraft and flight in general, skilled pilots who could share exciting war stories were seen as heroes. This popularity also led to the development of numerous series of planes throughout the course of the war.

Royal Air Force ace William Bishop, who is credited with more than seventy aerial victories in World War I, flew four different models of planes developed by Great Britain. Manfred von Richthofen, also known as the "Red Baron," was the German Air Force's most distinguished pilot, and perhaps the most renowned pilot in history. He flew six different models of aircraft throughout the war, and recorded eighty aerial victories—the most of any pilot on either side.

Mass production of planes began around this time. By 1917, the first all-metal plane was built. In 1918, the United States started airmail service. After World War I, many pilots had a hard time making a living. They often did "barnstorming"—performing stunts in the air for a paying crowd.

In 1927, former mail pilot and barnstormer Charles Lindbergh took off in his plane the *Spirit of Saint Louis*. He flew just over 5,632 kilometers (3,500 miles) from Long Island, New York, to Paris, France, in the first nonstop solo flight across the Atlantic. It took him 33 1/2 hours. When he landed, he became a hero and was called "the Lone Eagle." Thousands came to watch him land.

Lindbergh posing with *The Spirit of Saint Louis*

Chapter 4

By World War II, the race to make bigger, faster, and deadlier fighter planes was on between the Allies and Axis powers. In fact, the war on the United States started when Japanese bombers destroyed ships in Pearl Harbor, in Hawaii. Huge ships functioned as airplane carriers, so fighter pilots could take off right from the ships.

During World War II, plane technology made big advancements. The Germans invented jet engines, including the powerful Messerschmitt Me 163 Komet, which could go up to 965 kilometers (600 miles) per hour. The British developed radar (an acronym for RAdio Detection And Ranging), which sensed where planes were. Americans developed the massive Flying Fortress, or B-17, which could fly in high altitudes and carry many bombs.

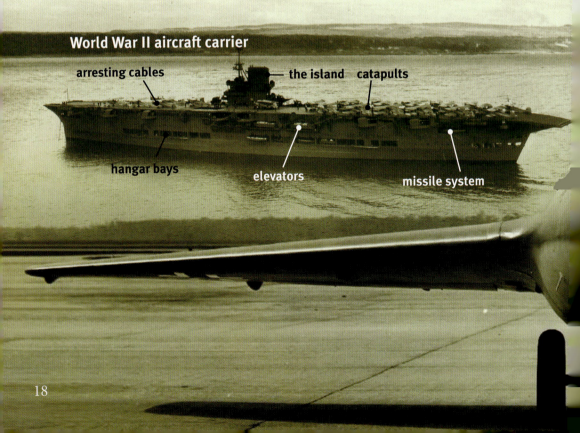

World War II aircraft carrier
arresting cables — the island — catapults
hangar bays — elevators — missile system

Experiments didn't end after the war. Nobody believed it was possible to fly faster than the speed of sound, but a band of U.S. Air Force pilots were determined to put this idea to the test. On October 14, 1947, Chuck Yeager broke the sound barrier for the first time, flying the rocket-powered Bell X-1 faster than 1,224 kilometers per hour (760 miles per hour).

The modern age of plane travel began in 1952. That's when the first jet-powered commercial plane, the de Havilland Comet, started carrying passengers. In 1970, the Boeing 747, one of the largest passenger planes ever built, started flying between London and New York. Able to carry more than 450 passengers, 747s are still flown today.

upper-deck lounge area of a Boeing 747 from the 1970s

The Messerschmitt Me 163 Komet was a rocket-propelled jet mass-produced in 1944.

Chapter 4

In 1976, the first commercial service for the **supersonic** plane began. The Concorde SST (supersonic transport) carried 100 passengers at twice the speed of sound, flying 50 percent faster than regular jet planes. But a deadly accident and high operating expenses grounded the Concorde by 2003. Since that time, commercial aircraft haven't changed much on the outside. But inside, they have become more fuel efficient and computerized, as well as quieter.

Military aircraft have also advanced. In the 1960s, the Lockheed SR-71 Blackbird, the fastest jet ever, started production. This spy plane flew for twenty-four years for the U.S. Air Force during the Cold War with the Soviet Union. Its final flight was in 1990, when it set a speed record. It flew from Los Angeles to Washington, D.C. in an astonishing one hour, four minutes, and twenty seconds. After that flight, the plane went to the Smithsonian's National Air and Space Museum, where it remains today.

The Concorde could fly from New York to Paris in about 3.5 hours.

How Planes Have Changed

The Nighthawk is also known as an F-117, and was formerly operated by the U.S. Air Force.

The Nighthawk is a modern stealth plane. These low-flying attack planes have massive delta (V-shaped) wings. Their covered engines give off little heat or noise. Special surfaces make them hard to see on radar.

Drones

Drones are one of the newest types of aircraft. Operated by remote control, drones are utilized to carry out espionage missions, as well as for combat. These unmanned aircraft are capable of carrying out missions that would normally put the lives of soldiers at risk while maintaining the accuracy and efficiency of being controlled by a real person.

Chapter 5

Beyond the Plane

Airplanes are not the only way that humans have taken to the skies. From gliders to hot-air balloons, humans have developed a number of ways to defy gravity. In the early 1900s, the German zeppelin was seen as an impressive feat of engineering, but within decades, humans would set their sights far beyond sailing among the clouds in a helium-filled balloon.

In 1900, a German count, Ferdinand von Zeppelin, built a better balloon. He put hydrogen gas balloons in a hollow, torpedo-shaped structure, held rigid by aluminum. Hydrogen is lighter than air, but it's also very flammable. Von Zeppelin added engines for power and fins for steering. Between 1911 and 1914, more than 1,600 zeppelin flights took place in Germany. After World War I, they became popular once again.

In 1937, a huge zeppelin, the *Hindenburg*, started flying over the Atlantic. It was more than 800 feet long and carried 7 million cubic feet of hydrogen. Its passengers traveled in luxury, reaching their destination in 3 days. But one tragedy destroyed the future of balloons as a form of travel. In 1937, the *Hindenburg* caught fire and crashed in New Jersey, killing 36 people (97 were aboard). The zeppelin's reputation was shattered.

The world became completely encompassed in a race to develop the most advanced technology to take people beyond Earth's atmosphere and help them uncover the mysteries of space. In the year 1969, a human set foot on the surface of the moon for the first time, a feat that just decades earlier would never have been deemed possible.

Technology has advanced even further since then. Countries have sent unmanned satellites deep into space, allowing for the discovery of countless stars and planets, some of which may be similar enough to Earth to sustain life. There are even rover units on Mars, allowing scientists to collect visual and physical data on the red planet.

photograph of the 1937 *Hindenburg* tragedy

Chapter 5

Helicopters

Helicopters can fly straight up, forward, backward, and laterally (side to side). They can land on almost any flat surface. They can also hover, or stay in one place in the air. Their many uses include tourism, rescue work, and traffic reporting. One of the biggest challenges of designing a "chopper," as the helicopter is often called, is figuring out how it can generate enough lift to go straight up, instead of relying on the thrust of forward motion that airplanes use.

The first helicopter was invented by Igor Sikorsky, an immigrant who came to the United States from Russia, in 1939. He developed the VS-300 helicopter for the U.S. Army. More than 130 had been built by 1942. His design included a large overhead rotor (a set of 4 overhead wings) at the top of the helicopter, and a small horizontal rotor on the side of its tail.

Igor Sikorsky in his VS-300

This sideways rotor spins in the opposite direction as the overhead rotor in order to fight against the twisting force called **torque**. If this didn't happen, the chopper would just spin around in circles. It couldn't be controlled. Many helicopters still have this design today.

view from a helicopter cockpit

Piloting a Helicopter

Helicopter pilots must be very agile. They have four controls. The cyclic, between the pilot's knees, is a hand control that moves the chopper forward or sideways. The collective, a hand control to the pilot's left, makes the helicopter move higher or lower. There are also two anti-torque pedals, one for each foot. They change the thrust of the tail rotor, so the nose moves in the direction of the pedal.

Chapter 5

Space Flight

Scientists worked long and hard to develop rockets powerful enough to go to outer space. The science of rocketry falls under the field of science that studies projectile movement, called **ballistics**. Moving objects straight up takes a tremendous amount of lift. To make it into deep space, an object must be propelled at 40,234 kilometers (25,000 miles) per hour! Because there is no oxygen in space, spacecraft have to carry their own oxygen to mix with their fuel. This adds even more weight that rockets must overcome.

In 1957, the Soviet Union sent the first satellite, called *Sputnik I*, into orbit. This began the space race between the Soviets and the Americans. The Soviet Union was the first nation to send a human into space, while the United States was the first, and remains the only, to land a human on the moon. Eventually, cooperation replaced competition. In the late 1990s, fifteen countries joined to create the International Space Station. Here, astronauts from around the world gather to do space experiments.

Beyond the Plane

International Space Station

The last man to walk on the moon was Eugene Cernan, December 1972. ▼

For many years, the United States used space shuttles for manned space trips. The shuttles were attached to giant rockets and fuel tanks that would fall away as the shuttle reached space. When the mission was completed, the shuttle could land like an airplane. The last shuttle was retired in 2012.

But space exploration is not over. Right now, missions like the Mars landers project, an exploration of the surface of the red planet, are still in progress. One mission planned for the near future includes looking for oceans on Jupiter's moon Europa. The quest to understand the universe continues.

Conclusion

Since the Wright brothers, plane designers have been planning for the future of aeronautics. Yet, most commercial planes today look much like the ones flown in the 1950s. That will most likely change in the future, for a variety of reasons. One reason is that the cost of fuel is rising. (The average price for a gallon of gas in the United States was 18 cents back in the 1950s.) Another is that people want to reduce plane noise and pollution. Finally, the number of air passengers keeps growing.

Designers consider all these factors when working on new planes. Boeing's SUGAR Volt is a design with extra-long, flexible wings that would allow for shorter takeoffs and require less power. Like the power systems in today's hybrid cars, the SUGAR Volt's system would combine fuel-burning engines, electric motors, and batteries.

Another aircraft currently in development is the N3-X. Its single, thick, triangular wing contains the cockpit, engines, and fuel tanks. It also features two thin wings on the sides of its wide body. This wing design is fuel efficient because the plane produces lift with its whole frame.

Other engineers are thinking about how they might catapult planes into the air, which would cut the energy needed for takeoff, or power planes with liquid hydrogen or solar energy. Though most of these designs are just ideas at this point in history, someday they may be our ticket to the open skies!

computer-generated rendering of Boeing's SUGAR Volt in flight

Glossary

aerodynamics	(air-oh-dy-NA-miks) *noun* a branch of study relating to the science of the motion of air and other gaseous fluids and with the forces acting on bodies in motion (page 4)
aeronautics	(air-oh-NAU-tiks) *noun* the study of flying through air (page 4)
ballistics	(buh-LIS-tiks) *noun* the science of projectile movement (page 26)
drag	(DRAG) *noun* a force on a plane that slows it down (page 9)
force	(FORS) *noun* a push or pull on an object that results from interacting with another object (page 8)
fuselage	(FYOO-seh-lahzh) *noun* the main body of an airplane (page 12)
gravity	(GRA-vih-tee) *noun* a force that pulls objects toward Earth (page 8)
lift	(LIFT) *noun* a force that fights against gravity and helps a plane stay in the air (page 5)
pitch	(PICH) *noun* the up-or-down angle of a plane (page 14)
supersonic	(soo-per-SAH-nik) *adjective* faster than the speed of sound (page 20)
thrust	(THRUST) *noun* a force that helps a plane move forward (page 9)
torque	(TORK) *noun* a twisting force around a specific point (page 25)
weight	(WATE) *noun* how much gravity pulls on something (page 9)

Index

aerodynamics, 4, 12
aeronautics, 4, 28
ballistics, 26
catapult, 29
Cayley, Sir George, 4, 8–9, 11
compressor, 14
da Vinci, Leonardo, 3
drag, 9, 11–13
force, 8–11, 14, 25
fuselage, 12
glider, 4–7, 16, 22
gravity, 8–10, 12, 22
Hindenburg, 23
hybrid, 28
hydrogen, 22–23, 29
International Space Station, 26
landing gear, 15
lift, 5, 9–11, 13, 24, 26, 28
Lilienthal, Otto, 3–6
Lindbergh, Charles, 17
pitch, 14
Poe, Edgar Allan, 2

satellite, 23, 26
Sikorsky, Igor, 24
Soviet Union, 20, 26
spoilers, 15
supersonic, 20
tail, 24–25
thrust, 9–10, 24–25
torque, 25
Verne, Jules, 2
weight, 9, 26
Wells, H. G., 2
Wright brothers, 4–7, 16, 28
Yeager, Chuck, 19
zeppelin, 22–23

Analyze the Text

Questions for Close Reading

Use facts and details from the book to support your answers to the following questions.

1. What are some factors that put the Wright brothers ahead of their competition in the early twentieth century?

2. Some early writers were wary of what would happen when aircraft developed. What were their fears, and were they correct in their fears? Use evidence from the text to support your answer.

3. How has war affected the development of aircraft?

4. Why is it more expensive and difficult to send a rocket into space than a plane into the sky?

Comprehension Skill: Analyze Text Structure

How does the author use chronological order to detail events in the text? Choose one section of the text that has a chronological structure. Use the chart to list details from the text in time order.

Page Numbers	Chronological Details